The Duende of Tetherball

THE **DUENDE** OF
TETHERBALL

TIM BOWLING

NIGHTWOOD EDITIONS

2016

Nightwood Editions
P.O. Box 1779
Gibsons, BC VON 1V0
Canada
www.nightwoodeditions.com

COVER PHOTOGRAPH: Nadia Westenburg
COVER DESIGN & TYPOGRAPHY: Carleton Wilson

Canada

 Canada Council Conseil des Arts
for the Arts du Canada
 BRITISH COLUMBIA
ARTS COUNCIL
An agency of the Province of British Columbia

Nightwood Editions acknowledges financial support from
the Government of Canada through the Canada Book Fund and
the Canada Council for the Arts, and from the Province of British Columbia
through the British Columbia Arts Council and the Book Publisher's Tax Credit.

This book has been produced on 100% post-consumer recycled,
ancient-forest-free paper, processed chlorine-free
and printed with vegetable-based dyes.

Printed and bound in Canada.

CIP data available from Library and Archives Canada.

ISBN 978-0-88971-325-3

CONTENTS

i.

The Children of Fishermen 11

The Duende of Tetherball 12

Boy to Man 14

School 16

Teaching Useless Skills to My Children 18

The Chain Smoker 20

The Poet 22

The Poor Relation 23

A Mother's Advice 24

Recovery 25

In Autumn 28

Arbutus 30

ii.

Teaching First-Year University 33

Telephone Survey 34

Advice to a Young Male Poet 36

Why I Move On Quickly from Critical Response 38

Whatever You Do 40

Ordinary Adult Day 42

Apology to Childhood 44

Crossroads 46

Our Animal Solitude 47

iii.

Coyote   55

Midlife, with Children   56

British Columbia   58

Roadkill Moose   60

Orcas   61

Midlife, on the Midway   62

The Changeling   64

Against the Haters   66

Classical   67

What Death Is   68

Alistair MacLeod   70

Twentieth Century Song   72

What I Owe   74

Acknowledgements   77

About the Author   79

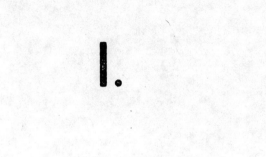

I.

THE CHILDREN OF FISHERMEN

Coal oil lanterns made us all town criers.
But what was there to cry for
lighting the gas lamps of consciousness
as we peered into the black depths
anticipating each death like a birth?

In our beds, we slept on swells
as if we actually rode the witches' broomsticks
of our dreams. At our schools'
show-and-tell
we showed driftwood –
the clumsy punctuation of the river's smooth sentence –
and told nothing. What did we know
that opening our mouths could tell?

We wore gumboots that glistened like the flanks of horses.
And slipped them off inside rain-rattled porches
as the salmon slipped off every tide.
We heard the glass floats being blown in Japan.
Our closest friends were dogs and blood.

Sometimes I look far and long into the dark
around my motionless bed
and it rises – my face, carved
out of my father's face –

but there is no one to show

and crying to a sleeping people
is a lonely way to tell.

THE DUENDE OF TETHERBALL

It isn't played much anymore. My kids don't play.
I don't play for nostalgia.
But well I remember that lump in the throat
of the agues of autumn
no day could swallow – on the schoolyard cement
in slanting rain, a scarecrow of iron
with its head lopped off, dangling, waiting
for some kid to smash it in the face
as if it were the abominated classroom clock
above the desks stalled in the hours
like our fathers' tractors in the muddied
potato fields so like their fathers' Passchendaele
they weren't alike at all.

You wrapped the leather ball
around the pole by punching it
against another's punches
or your own, a purely democratic
violence of the kind
the world teaches every one
of us, in time. Useless –
the monk setting fire to his flesh
to free his people
the grandmother chained to a Douglas Fir
to save a saw-whet owl's song
the writer of twenties noir
soldered to the keys of his Underwood
inspired by Joyce – useless.

Yet there's the tetherball in the compound.

A bully
who has no victim
but himself, a tree
stripped by acid rain,
a one-armed boxer with a single glove.

Did I say I didn't play? Who doesn't play?
In all weather, out there,
the tetherball says, "It's hard. Life's hard,"
and we get up from our stalled tractors
to punch above our weight
and the tetherball takes it and
gives it back – old confessor,
grounded bolt, imploded gourd

maypole of our solitudes and prison yard.

BOY TO MAN

I pick grade school's hopscotch game
up off the playground concrete's craquelure
of rain pocks and coupling
crane flies and go looking
for the boy who tossed his sister's
charm or a plucked dandelion head
against the wind and jumped
one-legged as a contemplative heron
into time. Can you help me?
Do you remember the rules
or perhaps the precise physics
of the toss, square to square,
the balance of the first bones
in the first winds? The delicate
release of the material
to faith?

Tucked under my arm, the game
without players
is the chalk outline
of the corpse in a murder case.
I carry my cold portfolio
under the cherry trees
stripped of blossoms
and, full of hope,
find only myself
a loved man who loves
awake at three a.m.
the crushed bones of a dove
in each hand the grist
off the white oars

I pushed off with –
where are the teachers
watching from the bank of windows
the coloured chaos on the compound?
Where is the chaos?

I put the game on the ground
mouth a number
toss the dust
and alone long after the bell

begin the jump that has no landing.

SCHOOL

The day I left the building for the last time
two blackboards tore off the walls and followed
one to either side
like wings, the shadows
of greater wings. I hunched
in their angled dark
Peter Lorre
in the pre-war German streets
hiding from the mob
among the crannied silhouettes
of buildings that housed
each inchoate Nazi.

Sometimes the chalk on the boards
would whisper old lessons:
You are small.
You are not free.
These were the equations
set out in a voice
the sound of mice-gnaw.

But mostly the chalk spelled my name
wrong and stayed silent.
Death. Time. Loss.
I couldn't look away.

Now I feel the vice
as the steer enters the stockyard
the Munch hands fly to my skull

I look straight at my children
and cry to my parents,
What have you done?

in my trembling hand
the chalk that writes the truth
on the air
and breaks.

To set a gillnet for salmon
turn the wheel so that the net,
rolling off the drum, rests
in loops on the water; the web,
then, will hang without stress,
securing the gill at the strike,
and never set within five fathoms
of either bank: deadheads
and other snags hug the margins.
Remember, the westerly that brings
fine weather does not generally bring fish
and makes setting a perilous task,
the web catching on the rollers
and ripping or, worse, wrapping
the prop as the stern drifts across.
Don't swing your gaff like a baseball bat:
you're not knocking apples off branches;
those silver bodies are your keep
and must be hooked
with a grandmother's care
at an heirloom rug.

As for a life lived in metaphor
as if metaphor is blood and breath
the beauty of the world
made more beautiful
by always being something else,
you might as well accept your heart
as the flower laid in the tomb
of the chest you carry everywhere
over rivers and banks of purple cinquefoil
searching for the end of searching
to find only the face of the world
on the world's face
– a radiant blankness –
the poet's epitaph.

THE CHAIN SMOKER ,
   for Russell and Aaron Thornton

My oldest son – still a boy, almost a man – laughs,
"Were you a player, Dad?" looking at my high school
graduation photo. Immediately I see past myself
to the grade nine dropout salmon fisherman
who donned a rumpled grey suit jacket to drive
the rented Lincoln town car that took us
to the dance. He smoked one brand
of cigarettes – over a pack a day –
from the age of fourteen. Player's.
It had a smiling sailor on the carton
and he had been a smiling sailor
in the war, when he met my mother
who would be his only girl
for sixty years. He would joke,
"A sailor has a girl in every port.
Your mother really got around."

I used to try and smoke
my candy cigarettes
with Popeye the sailor
man on the pack
in time to his inhales.
I can still taste the sugar on the air
if I try, and I don't have to try.

My arm that night
made a smoke ring around my date
in the backseat the chauffeur's
blue glance in the rear-view mirror
meets my blue glance
thirty years later. And mine
meets my son's. And will
thirty years later. I smile
over the ghostly *V* in my hand.
"No. I was never a player."

Swallowing the sweet of the inhale.

THE POET

He was born crying and he died laughing.
And in between? Some smiles
given mostly to the old,
the young, women. And he wept
at the still swings in schoolyards
knowing the god had risen
from the stirrups of a dead mount.

Grass on the one cheek,
grave-dirt on the other
it was never clear to us
why he turned the grass to the rain
the dirt to the sun
but the breath was sweet
that commissioned the words.

I say this for him
who would have said it better:
the growl in a dog
the blood in a killdeer
the bullet hole on each side
of the salmon's grace

became the rope of seeing
from which his body hangs
white as the sheet of the world
the parents sleep on, nightmared,
caging the human cries in bone.

THE POOR RELATION

My cousin's death remains mysterious.
Schizophrenic, off his meds, homeless,
he either did or didn't take refuge
in some Dutch farmer's stable from the deluge
that bled wide the black sloughs' arteries.
If he did, then, it's entirely possible, yes,
the horse kicked him in the chest,
stopping his heart, then in the head.
If he didn't, clearly he was killed
by person or persons unknown, taken
and dumped in the foul straw, a broken
scarecrow stuffed with blood.

Both of his parents are long since dead.
His twin's in prison. I'm the only cousin
left who wonders if it (no, not that)
behooves us to gather perhaps together
in a clan and … well, I guess not.
Better to leave the sad fact mysterious,
though I remember, in another time,
long before the drugs and dislocation,
Kenny on the courthouse steps
wrapped a bandana around his head
like an intestine
and protested the Americans' entry into Laos.

A MOTHER'S ADVICE

Always wash your hands after handling money –
who knows who's touched it before you?
Whenever you go into the city,
even on the hottest summer days,
wear long pants – it's a matter of respect.
Do not eat the seeds in an apple –
they're poisonous. Arrive
ten minutes before doctor's appointments –
you might get in early. Remember:
if a girl has slim ankles,
she's more likely to keep her figure.
Waste not want not. When buying
cantaloupe, scrape and sniff the rind
for freshness. Be polite – you can attract
more flies with honey than with vinegar.
Self-approval is no recommendation.
Never keep tomatoes in the fridge.
Write thank-you notes.
Respect your elders.
Wear clean underwear whenever
taking a trip by car or plane –
if there's an accident, you don't
want to be embarrassed.
Do unto others as you would
have them do unto you.

Don't die before me

please

don't die before me.

Ill but on the mend, the children,
home from childhood (will they ever
be so again?) play
the board games of my youth.
All day, through the haze
of half sleep, I hear them
rooms away, cry *Trouble*
and *Sorry*, *Sorry* and *Trouble*
the Irish condolence
when the sickness only ends
in death – *Sorry for your trouble*
spoken in mist, softly as mist –
and the whole house rolls
like dice through the years
gathering dog fur and old
birthday cards, pulled-off
Band-Aids from the wounds
that healed (no protection
for what cuts the father
now). My next move
is to rise. Outside

the neighbourhood is everywhere
back alleys the colour of sperm whales,
backed onto by garages, dishevelled,
the doors like well-worn dungarees –
above every third or fourth one
a basketball hoop, no longer used,
the players moved away, the nets
either melted like snow or
dangling in shreds (to catch

the invisible carp?). The evening
grows old, gazed at
through these sad vaudevillian eyes
with the dark shadows underneath
I grow old, waiting for the fall-back
jumper of the rising moon to fall.

It never does, of course. But always
the promise of promise
leads us on, illness to health,
the simple game with the simple rule
and then the darker game
we have to invent ourselves
and play alone, no longer sorry
for anyone's troubles
except this world's.

Returned to the yard, to the remnant
of the snowman made out of the last snow
by my youngest child
who had to be coaxed
to perform what had once been joy
and who will not make again
a semblance life from the fabric
of the planet's turning
until perhaps he helps to make
a new maker, his hands that
held the snow, the bouncing ball,
that hold the die,
one day opened to hold the child
already whispering the rules
in another room
so as not to disturb his father.

The house is there. Go in.
The love is there. And yet
I cannot bear to leave him
next year's snowman
the one who will not be made.
He is like a son to me
the one we did not make together
when there was still time.

I see him
standing where winter is
no words on his mouth of stone
not Sorry or Trouble
just the eyes of coal
that don't close
but keep filling
dark after dark

as night falls through the hoops
on the eyelids of the sleeping parents
on the wintry stare of generations

blazing their accusatory spark into the earth.

Geese are tearing like roof tiles off a scoured-pan sky.
And I am afraid to die.

All twilight long
I sit in the car in the driveway
still driving
my teenaged daughter's shuddering shoulder blades
in my hands.
Why is my wisdom of no use to the young?

Forty years ago
a man by a backyard fire
waits for the wood to turn to ash
so he can go to bed.
He pokes the embers with a cut branch
fishing on the lip of the volcano.

It isn't the loss as much as the leaving
that burns.

"I spy with my little eye,"
I used to say to my little ones,
"something that is…
mortal."

"Is it you, Daddy? Daddy, it's you!"

"Yes, it's me."

My twelve-year-old cries, friendless,
"Dad, no one gets my references."

His older brother says, home late,
"Sorry, I lost all track of time."

Now the small, missing motor
of a Canada goose goes over,
the sound of the past – not mine,
the planet's – and I look out,
alone with the old references
untracked but moving
the car a kind of probe
set out to find
signs of life where millions already live

my two hands,
stranger, just like yours,
starfish on the margins blurred
relentlessly with tears.

ARBUTUS

Gallows tree for the sunset
and closet for the summer tans
of city children who turn back
on the ferry's deck
to see the Spanish silhouette
crouched in warm salt dark.

All along the coast
on the elemental edge
where seals grease the swell
and kelp beds pass
in a confusion of cords and plugs
humming to a low green power
these battered lighthouses
shine from within
each manned by a sole cormorant,
a comma in the pages of history.

Holding moonlight like a plunged corpse
yet they fire the veins with life,
their bark gentled to the slippery pulp
as a newborn to the mother's breast.

Rain only deepens our pleasure in their colour.

Deer skin, salmon flesh, human blood.
My faith hangs on a vivid rood.

II.

At first I felt sorry for myself –
for having to be there, for the need
to pay the mortgage, for the pigeon-like
filling of the pigeon holes. Then
I felt sorry for them – for having
to be there, for the need to shatter,
or at least adjust, the chrysalis,
the hearing of an invisible owl
calling a name that won't
be theirs for years. At last,
I didn't feel sorry at all.

If a rainbow were to shatter
at your feet, and you picked
it up, some of the colours
would burn, some would soothe,
some would sink into your skin,
others would blind you

but it would all be rainbow
and you would stop for it –

what else should you do?

TELEPHONE SURVEY

No one tells the truth about truth
– Adrienne Rich

Do I want others to be like me?
No.
Would the world be a better place
if they were?
Yes.
So, I do not want the world
to be a better place. From my cells
less hatred, more compassion,
respect for women, children,
animals – no violence, pornography,
paving over of watersheds –
more of the dark between stars
more of the silence between words
each day saddled like an old horse
each night groomed with velvet hands.
From the blood my parents
gave me
a tolerance requiring no gods
a curiosity needing no devices:
when I look up
a comfortless infinity
when I look down
grass that I can touch
and divide for the grave.
In autumn the rotting peach light
on the rusted wheelbarrow astonishes.
In winter the popped champagne
bottle of the bald eagle in the firs

celebrates humility.
Armed men will no longer walk the earth
picking up the dark laundry
of the flocks they have scattered,
awe will craft to replicate,
love will be as the seasons –
changeable but constant –

and death when it comes
will be death

yet I do not want all other selves
to be this self.

I would have my children live
with the terrifying risk of difference
to the precipice of tragedy
to the obliteration of the meaning
of my days

for it is a crime to command life:
and the prison is a mirror that shows a single face.

ADVICE TO A YOUNG MALE POET

Auto shop. They were hoisting by winch
a 351 Cleveland engine block
out of some grade twelve's
two-tone Mustang ragtop.
I was half my gender away
across the oil-puddled parking lot
and a scabrous soccer pitch
reading *Macbeth* and looking up
at the dangled car part
the size and colour
of a typewriter or
the Thane of Cawdor's
murderous heart:
"Aroint thee, witch."

Fifteen, scared but still apt
to toss "damn thee black
thou cream-faced loon"
in PE class at the rippling back
of some hoop or net-bound jock,
I was learning – too soon –
the only lesson that counts:
how to be alone.

It was May. But August hot.
I could feel the purple in the lilacs
spreading bruises under the sun.
The swing on a long chain in the park
swung slightly with the weight
of some Victorian ghost,
a stray dog on its hobo mission
paused to give me the custard eye
but decided (out of camaraderie?)
not to bark. A leathery raven
landed on the grass to make the most
out of a lunch-hour sandwich
wrapped in wax. "Macbeth doth murder sleep,"
I read in the beat-up Signet paperback edition
with essays by A.C. Bradley and Samuel Johnson
before I let the copy drop in my lap.

When I woke –
thirty years of work
at the old hunt and peck
on my hunched back,
my hands slick
from the oily block –
the lesson wasn't over
though there wasn't any teacher
and nothing else to learn.

Welcome to Scotland, brother.

WHY I MOVE ON QUICKLY FROM CRITICAL RESPONSE

Sometimes I'm asked what it's like to be a poet.
Okay, I'm never asked. And that's mostly what it's like.
But it's also this:

the autumn I turned fifteen,
I worked on a potato combine –
eight teens bent over a conveyor belt
four to each side
tossing out the clumps of mud and culls.
My god, I was so happy in that air
on that land, the smell of rain, the sunlight
the colour and sheen of a retriever's fur
and then the first velour descent of dusk
our hands pale and quick
under the electric lights
as the machinery hummed over the earth's hum.
I began to sing – just to myself – my work
easy, in synch, rhythmic.
I spied and hucked the culls with flair.
As we crept along the rows, from time to time,
I looked up to see I was being mocked,
my singing and my gestures aped,
grossly, to the merriment of all.

I was fifteen. I stopped.
We reached the end of the field.
The tractor shuddered and shut down.
The laughter and the snickering
subtly unsubtle
as is common to that age
crept on
for days
until a new target hove
into view and I
was left alone.

It hurt. It hurt me in the place
I didn't know I could protect.
What right had I – have I – to joy?

Now I go out alone in the dawn cold
to start the frozen tractor
and sit in the hard, icy seat
staring at the black rows
whose crop is never certain
and feeds only the few.

Yet my joy is the joy
of the gulls
following the crab fishermen home
from their long labours
with the muscles and salts
of the eye and the sea.

Do not take the time to write a letter to your mother.
Do anything else. Anything.
Correct the comma splices and fragments
in a stack of thirty-seven undergraduate papers
on "A Rose for Emily" by William Faulkner.
Transfer your vinyl LPs to CDs
to digital back to vinyl
while muttering "B-side," "concept album," "long player,"
and shedding a tear
for each loss of every RCA Victor
Volt Stax and Hot Wax
all the turntable memory
spin it, groove your needle, relax
– my god – do anything, anything else.
Perform open heart surgery
on a Rufous hummingbird with
the tweezers from the game of
Operation you last played
with the babysitting neighbour girl
in those primitive pre-mobile
device years all those – *bzzz* –
years ago – *bzzz* – anything.
Just don't write a letter to your mother.

Gather together a donation of sweaters
to stuff in a garbage bag and leave
on the stoop (marked B for the Big Brothers)
so that when they pull up in their rumbling truck
to collect your threadbare and otherwise out-of-favour wool
you can get up from your roll-top at the clamour
and forget all about writing a letter to your mother.

Do anything else. It doesn't matter.
The age demands that you do something better
than hang from the monkey bars
of some useless haunting childhood hour
that no one else can ever really understand
now that you no longer have a father.
Whatever you do
do not take the time to write a letter to your mother.

She's old. Soon the final petals of her pulse will fall
and the songbirds she always whistled to her feeder
will have to fly without that sonar
and so will you, and so will I,
so why
why bother
why take the time to…

you'll still find the boxes to tick on the tax forms
you'll gape and mutter like a little boy
when your wife informs you that your daughter
has bled for the first time
in the month your mother breathed for the last
you'll get up, lie down, get up,
and finally never get up at all

your eyes full, not with pain – no –
but with every singular inessential
second you had your children as children in your life.

Ordinary adult day
with the blue devils of nada.
Don't go under. Tread the tepid water.
Looking across the narrow river channel of childhood
at the tall registration numbers
on the forearms of the fishboats
946 – part of my first girlfriend's
phone number (she died of breast cancer
ten years ago – the breasts I longed
to touch, and never touched) – I put my hands
in the kadaifi dough of the mourning Greek mother
across the street
whose eldest son drowned so far off the coast
they never found him – her black sleeves in the flour –
don't go under! Tread the tepid water!
Was it the winter of '76
we were all so keen
to watch, past midnight,
The Summer of '42?
How innocent our innocence.
Those boys – Danny and Blair and Vaughn –
a world of wet dreams and
first erections, GI Joe in fatigues
on the dresser top, the glued
model Tiger Moths still hanging
from their twines –
and as the boy in the film
steadied the ladder for the young war widow
his trembling hands suddenly on her hips
how were we to know
holding our breath

that the blue devils would find us
here at the half-century
where the sun lowers itself
on the plangent horizon
and every boat
leaving the harbour
rolls the same slow credits
as a tombstone
to tell the story of ordinary time?

APOLOGY TO CHILDHOOD

I have failed to advance the cause.
A voice cries out in the suburbs:
Where is the off-leash area for the human?
I have not encouraged the heart from the nest.

It should be the simplest thing in the world.
Before the rain, the sidewalks' colour was porridge.
After the rain, chocolate.
The fallen blossoms of the cherry
carved little spoon dips
all the mile of our way to school
where the desks in the classroom,
unlike the fishboats in the harbour,
did not move, except from one year's
obedience to another's; our teachers
chamoised chalk from the board,
our fathers hosed blood
from the deck. On the sheet-metal sea
the slick pod of orcas' backs
dropped like the roller coaster
down the first steep decline
and the seagulls screamed.

What have I ever done to offer you the day of your birth?
When the buskers play, too often I drop tears in the case.
At the daffodil's bloom, the beat cop's flashlight finds the corpse.

It is no comfort to be unalone in my weakness.
The widow-makers in the rainforest fall and
form a crèche for the infant Despair.
Van Gogh's eyes blaze in every salmon
that splashes the oils of the spawn on the leaves
and we are not there.

I have watched the great blue heron
lift the lid of one casket, then the other,
searching for a child's face
in the dark rain, the sideways rain,
the rain that tastes of salt and creosote,
and my heart has tightened with the eagle's talon

because the present must always feed –
like a lizard – on live prey

and I have failed to keep the past alive for you.

In the effort lies the honour?
It is not what I wanted.

What good is our honour
if the wood won't burn

if the phoenix will not fire?

CROSSROADS

Was it birdsong today
that turned me to the poems
of Edward Thomas
or the poems of Edward Thomas
that turned me to birdsong?

I am a middle-aged Canadian male
with three children and a mortgage
and a long relationship with a river
that ended badly
and I am always between –

birth and death
the mind and heart
courage and fear –

and the one keeps turning me
back to the other
until poetry is birdsong
and every morning through the open windows
of the rooms where I look in upon my sleeping children
the first singers sing
of the rain and the path
through the woods, autumn
smoke and always
the lattermath to my hoar spring.

OUR ANIMAL SOLITUDE

Even the sun is roadkill to our speed.
Dead at the peripheries. Toss its soft carcass
to the grass already stained
with red sheddings
from previous leaps. Scroll
down drive on. Plenty more days
where days come from.
Once, on my haunches,
facing the splattered grille,
I picked the meat from between
the snoring giant's teeth
as the eyes of other creatures
rife as plankton
drifted in the black surf
between the pines
and the moon, scalded
in the tryworks, took hours
to sink. Wolf breath. And
every river's raised hackles.
Now – who stops? Only
the choiceless, ripped
without anaesthetic
from the womb.

She had an appointment in the Fort.
Saskatchewan. Forty minutes east
of Edmonton. As the crow flies.
And there were no crows flying.
Minus forty with wind chill.
Shag carpet of hoarfrost on the branches,
the highway a hooked cuirass.

An ordinary woman of the late middle years. Once, on her bedroom wall, she had a Donny Osmond poster. She listened to Casey Kasem and the Billboard Top 40 on a transistor radio. She had a brand-new pair of roller skates and she had a brand-new key. Her parents – wedded during the War. Big bands – Glenn Miller and Tommy Dorsey. Split when she was ten. Six schools in two provinces over the next four years. One unwanted pregnancy at sixteen. Miscarried. Moved out of her mother and stepfather's home at seventeen. Quit school. Lived with boyfriend for two years. Waitressed. Partied. Got sick and tired of her life. Returned to school for high school diploma. Worked in retail. Didn't date for a few years. Met first husband through a friend. One good decade. Two kids – one by caesarean, one epidural. A bad three years. Divorced. Earned real estate licence. Top seller five years running. Always running. Kids and clients – herself last. Holidays in Mexico. Mother died. Father died. Met second and current husband. His second marriage. One stepdaughter. Who hated her. Took up running. Vinyl to Walkman to iPod. Elton John and ELO. Worked. Worried. Survived breast cancer scare. Stepdaughter came around. All three kids graduated. Helping with tuition. In love with husband but physical desire waning. Many friends. Much laughter. Some tears. Texts arriving with a bleep. Cell phone rings to Annie Lennox singing "Here Comes the Rain Again." Sometimes imagines the smell of breast milk and the gurglings of her babies. Imagines grandchildren. Is mostly grateful. And always in a hurry. Foot down on the gas into the oil-black Alberta night.

Then the black is bricked –
smashed glass, heart smashed,
as if a meteor, God's fist,
struck and tried to catch
the shards and sprays of blood
as her flailing foot lifts
to brake against the icy ditch
but hangs, as her head hangs,
loose, divorced from breath
if not her neck, which flames
bellowed by terror –
the roadkill animal in her chest,
crouched to follow, remains,
wild panic reduced to pants – alive!
The car is still
at last, spun out, upright
off the other shoulder
on the grass – one headlight's
silver creek bed growing cold
with dying fish – the engine's
far-off star-hum whitely calm –
she learns to be herself again.

But who can be the self – the vanished self –
with the dying buck's head
gashed and twisting in your lap,
the antlers pinning you behind the wheel
each short rasp torn from punctured lungs
and one eyeball glistening like an ocean mussel
as the car fills with a tide of blood smell
and you twist your own head in the lap
of space and all its colliding indifferent matter?

It's a lonely stretch of highway there, and the few vehicles at night travel too fast to want to stop, especially in winter. She couldn't reach her cell to call for help – the antlers like hardened straps on an electric chair held to the end of whatever purpose had to be served by the animal's slow dying and her tearful observance of its trial. Later, after the shock and fear diminished, she said the worst part was, just when the poor creature's suffering seemed over, it gave another wrenching breath and sudden twist in its collar of shatter. By then, her bloodied lap and the all-but-severed head had made her think of birth – she had hours to think, of course – and not-birth, the saddest moment of her past, returned – not to accuse, because she had done no wrong, since to follow the body and the confused heart had been no fault, but to comfort, which almost made it worse. She wasn't a foolish woman – she isn't now – and she had lived more than a half-century to learn that living is hard enough that never being born might in some sense be a gift. How are we to know? Except she wanted only life herself, and for her loved ones, and if she could have gone back and slowed the car or sped it up to save the animal's life, she would certainly have done so. In the end, in the last hour, before help arrived, she felt composed enough to stroke the chamois fur around the great black eye; she even sang a little, so she said in the telling, then looked away, as if she could hear a voice the rest of us couldn't hear, or maybe she was a little embarrassed that she'd been chosen for the privilege of living-in-death while another being died-in-life. Myself, I might have felt a different substance in my eyes than simply human tears – maybe living well means that you come to cry the blood of animal suffering before you're given your own release. But that's only speculation at a distance a great deal shorter than what she travelled that night. And she was carrying ghosts.

In the end, the trucker who finally stopped, who shook his own bear's head and bearish bulk as he brought her back – physically and all other ways – to the coordinate world, bluntly put the matter in perspective. "It's a nice buck," he said. "Too bad you can't eat it. The meat's bruised."

COYOTE

Shoved its head heraldic
through the autumn foliage fifty
feet along the winding
trail, just around the corner
of my fiftieth year. Crashed
my leashed dog's blood and
bones, crashed my half century
of what was and what's to come –
didn't even turn to look,
ghost face pushing through the plaster
of the ancestral manse
microbe under the microscoping sun
then – on a three count – stone
on the surface of a pool, slipped under, gone.

So the present erases also the real
not just the imagined or recalled.

What am I here, to the time that stops?
I pull my feral moment from the page
eyes red with the incendiary
subtraction
the sound of a half-starved running
at the far end of the telescope.

MIDLIFE, WITH CHILDREN

One responsibility now: existence.
Leave the flowering of the self to others:
the young, the immature, those all-hours
connivers still suckling
the wizened teat of the romance
of the ego of the artist. Skeptical
of religion, I nevertheless
lack the lip to sneer
at generation, blood, the royal
succession of the common line.
The bible's begats and body's knowings
slice choice off the bone of God
too hard to swallow – we go before,
we come after. All the trivia
of our wants, the tiresome pleas
for the world's attention: kill them
with each stroke of the pen
or enter the silence as the wings' colour
its cocoon. Montaigne's view
that the aging have no right
to hoard their wealth
from the young speaks only
to the property we can buy and sell:
I speak of a different coin,
what the female salmon spends
in the creek of her origin
as she defends her eggs
in their fragile redd of gravel
with her fungal suppurating flesh
and starved ascetic's eyes
for a week, two weeks,

for as long as her existence lasts:
that responsibility, that faith,
that terrifying wilderness.

The smell of burnt toast
indicates a coming stroke.
The smell of charred salmon, then?
The death of childhood?

I woke, gasping, from a dream.
Instead of sockeye in the hold
of my father's boat –
golden retrievers, their throats cut.
I had to take them by the fur
and cram them in the side lockers.
They were heavy, and did not slide
on their oils. The bared teeth
in the death-grins seemed human
but the black, unyielding stare
and contusions of flies
remembered ten thousand salmon
and a hundred years
of gaff work. But they were dogs,
and weighed as much as me
at ten. The odd one breathed.
I had to use the club we used for seals.
Then, the river flowing around the boat
proved another artery to be cut,
the clouds coagulant at the wound
in the flesh between worlds.
I woke when I recognized the family pet.

And immediately wanted to run in the rain
over soaked grass for penance
the bloodied ends of leashes in my hands
ten thousand dogs turning back
on their owners with a growl,
on their god, whatever their god is,

and me, running,
who has no god, and never will,
unless it is these years
I turn back on
and take in my arms
and store at my father's direction

unless it is these years.

ROADKILL MOOSE

Small arms cache for terrorists?
Butt ends and barrels of rifles
sticking out at odd angles.
We don't stop we slow down
a little nothing stops us little slows
us down we look and speed up
capture the carcass on the phone
to share and post and place
a giant Scot's haggis of bagpipe
stuffed with sound blown
for the last time

as two ravens like Othello's shoulders

descend on the snowy innocence.

ORCAS

They die like Victorian women
unhinged by one stillbirth too many.
But once in the Gulf of Georgia
they rose all around me
like cliffs of *The Prelude*.
Not to be climbed.
Not to be mastered.
The years we've lived.
The years ahead.

MIDLIFE, ON THE MIDWAY

When the roustabouts set about
assembling the haunted
house
I offered help.

If it's ghosts you're after
I can construct the coldest laughter.

They wrenched another lug and
looked
away.

And where they looked
is the midway where
every game of chance
involves the chancy self and
doubt.

Have you done all you could
to pay down the mortgage
you took out
on who you thought you'd be
ten thousand recess bells ago?
Toss a ring.
Can you look all your childhood
photos in the face?
That crazy hall of mirrors
has a hundred exits
and but a single
choice.
Sorry, kid. Try again.

With the bearded lady's beardless son
I make my end-of-summer pact:
to put all the kernels from the popcorn
that didn't pop
and lay scattered on the grass
in an envelope and
hope.
But August is no address for the post.
Even the kids of the freaks won't write back.

Now the Ferris wheel has paused
its final time – no one's on
but a boy of ten. The red sun
sloshes from all the other seats
and stains the metal chains
and shadows on the ground.
The operator at the lever
looks like me, or any man
who's reached the end of work,
of years of work, and looks
briefly at the sky to see
a pair of sneakered feet
dangling, and gasps, and
feels his brow, and thinks,
"For a second there, I thought…
the part of life that, living first,
was living most, I thought…
where is my mind
that isn't lost?"

and cranks the bar
to bring his midlife's
only issue
down.

THE CHANGELING

When my face became a spider's web
I still had to work I still had to live:
no accommodation for fragility
no dispensation for my radiance.

I walked out in the world with an alien hunger
and a human agency.
The wind on the bare nerves of my expression!
How could I hold so much light and not break?

The first looks of horror, and the first flies,
caught and made a maelstrom of my artistry.
I swallowed the loathing and I swallowed the life
and my face sagged a little – like a soldier's
in a shelled village – and darkened
but only as stained glass darkens
with the dust and soot of centuries.

I found it best to stand slightly
to the side
of endeavour
observing with my sensitivity
to touch asking
do I have the right to consume the weak
because they cannot avoid my terror?

By day's end, sated with the dumb blood
of each scorched planet stalled in my orbit
I began to see the respect in men's eyes.
They studied me for my mechanics.
They admired me for my guile.
One or two quietly tried to wring
a great tear of the sun
from my eyes
without making me blind.

All night, I held the moon
like a great moth
in my smile.

But shortly after dawn
a child touched my face in wonder

and I was gone.

What is it like to be seventeen?
My son gets up, goes to school, goes to work, goes to bed.
Hey Dad, how was your day? The Leafs traded Kessel.
But what is it *like*? Hand on the door to the self.
Not yet thinking about thinking. I was there – once –
now I'm here. And I know only that the culture
lies about youth to get even for losing it.
Sex is on the mind of the middle-aged
who make the movies
more than it's on the mind
of the young. Drink a glass
of water, laugh, look at your phone,
look at a girl. Simply do what the world
gives you to do
every minute. Or don't.
You are the lead in the pendulum
and both points of the arc
and the motion –
the stuffed animal can't be thrown out
or the grandmother's death imagined.
Though speed is your air
and distraction your meat
yours is a natural Buddhism.
The hum that comes off your solitude
from the lightly struck gong
in your chest – I hear it
but Time has buried that god
for me. Even so, godless
as I am, I will not
join the ironic choirs of the world that resent
the sincerity of your body's residence in song.

CLASSICAL

I bid my busking son
to rosin a bow
carved from a coyote's rib
and to play the Old World
with the New.
That music failed.
It was a screeching sound
as of a train grinding
to a stop
while murdered gypsies
in the forest
stared out from their fur.
Sparks shivered off my son's intensity.
He held his head to one side.
He might have been asleep
on the filthy pillow of Europe.
He might have been a totem
tilted in the rain.
At last the bow dissolved
like a child's knuckle
under Baba Yaga's pestle

to crematorium smoke
to sweat lodge vapour

to nothing but a cold cloud of breath
the wary coyote takes again

as it howls goodbye to the human forever.

WHAT DEATH IS

for Philip Levine (1928–2015)

I keep expecting another letter from you.
Dear Tim. I died on Valentine's Day. It sucks.
But the mailman passes by
like a deer in the middle of the night
with shredded paper on its antlers
like a boy driving his father's car
the trunk filled with crumpled
beer cans and union pamphlets
the headlights shedding a century's
worth of cigarette smoke.

Phil, the moon is in a long eclipse
but only over one country:
the nation of words
words that begin as cities
(exciting, dark, dangerous)
turn into rooms
(familiar, warm, close)
and become, at the end,
merciless and alien as space.

Yours smell of exhaust, fire,
the rosin on antique Russian violins,
and a brother's sweat. The earth
that pushes up through them
is from the rebel's makeshift grave
and the mock-orange's birth.
I press my face close
my fingers reading the Braille of all blindness
but it isn't the same. You, who hated

lies, would hate the lie
that art is the essence of a life.
It is only the residue. And yet
each word came from a factory
without bosses
in a world full of workers
and weighs as much
as an engine block
or an anchor carved
out of Jewish eyes.

Phil, however much I want you alive
is not even a fraction of the amount
you would want your life back
the poems unwritten
the forge's heat in your face

and yet
the mailman still passes by
the deer still carries each season to the depth of the woods
and the frightened little boy with the key to power
follows the beams without mercy over the border beyond
speech.

ALISTAIR MACLEOD

A cheer rose up from the scattered ranks of that losing army
(Canadian writers who write about Canada)
when we heard that you'd taken the ridge
and won a blasted acre of the world's acclaim.

I don't remember now
if you died before or after
Scotland voted against freedom
and in the tired eyes of the world
it seems to matter less
than when the pipes screeched at Culloden
or when, young in Windsor,
you finished "The Boat"
at your office desk,
but how amused you always were
that Scotland tried to claim you
as a native son. No great mischief,
I suppose, if the maple leaf should fall
off the tartan of your clan,
though if that twinkle in your eyes
belonged to anyone, it belonged
to the god of the season of the long sentence who painted grey
the tombstone whales and lowered the rattling craftsman's cage
deeper into the earth
than Jules Verne ever dreamed
of descending.

It seems only fitting, this almost-Christmas night,
that I read from a paperback copy
of your salt blood book
while my free hand rests
on the muzzle of the family dog:
her breathing, my pulse, the rhythm
of your words
must be the ancestors of the spirit
of the son you lost, and always mourned, if anything is.

Two stories: the one, twice-told
to me, in hotel lobbies, at festivals, over years,
how you once delivered milk in glass bottles
by horse-drawn wagon in Edmonton's
meat-locker cold – the frozen cream
at the neck a kind of miniature
Cape Breton floe-jammed strait;
the other, in your last letter,
of how proud you were of Alexander,
"a fine writer and even finer
man." I saw a whole coastline
surging with blood, kelped with sentences,
when I looked to the east

as I look again now, through the snows
which fall the same all over the earth,
missing the living presence of the national poet

who meticulously translated all of his poems into prose.

Why do I love silent film so much?
Because so many I loved are now silent.
The gesture and look, the electric touch,
remind me of my father, favourite uncle and aunt,
even our small-town baker as pale as his dough
who has for years leavened only the grass, and his old
Labrador retriever who lay on the cobblestones outside
the shop on sunny days and rose and settled like sifted
flour whenever a customer came
and darkened as if spiced when it rained.

Mr. Mayer. Joe. Joe Mayer. He was Dutch.
And had a faint blue tattoo near his wrist
rarely seen because he always moved
his hands so fast. His dog... I can see
its grizzled muzzle, and smiling, friendly face
with the rubbery licorice lips. Jiggs.
Yes, that was it. I remember the day
my mother sent me to buy a loaf of raisin bread
and Jiggs wasn't there, and the baker
who always had a kind word for kids
didn't speak and took the coins like nails
into his hand and didn't speak
and held his hand out with the change
for long seconds, and for once
I saw the long blue string of numbers
exposed like a vein at his wrist
and waited for the coins to break
in my hand
and the tears in his eyes to break.
But neither did.

Someone somewhere – for half a breath –
in the dark booth
behind the oven's golden light
changed the childhood reel
to this reel
and now I watch and love
every image remaining
until my warm body rises
and my children must break it for bread.

WHAT I OWE

My father was a fisherman. I admired him.
In the freshet's rage, he unwebbed each salmon
with the same care he took needling
a splinter from my palm. Silence
was his only curse.

My mother stayed home. I admired her.
She reached always into the kitchen cupboard
of her heart and never
found it bare. Hummingbirds
mistook her for a flower.

Together, for half a horrible century,
they were patience and stillness,
tending hives in a lightning storm;
they were river and ocean
blended but always themselves.

The sewing needle in the kettle's steam
her hand
the sewing needle in my skin
his hand

around me cupping my life to its end.

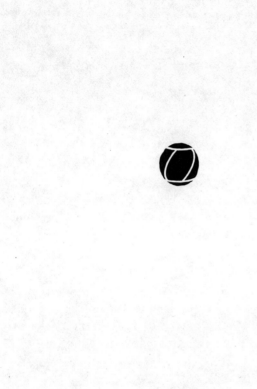

ACKNOWLEDGEMENTS

Several of these poems first appeared in *Queen's Quarterly*, *Fiddle-head*, *Arc* and *Maisonneuve*. "The Duende of Tetherball" also appears in *Best Canadian Poetry in English 2016*. My appreciation to the editors. I also wish to thank the Edmonton Arts Council for its support in the writing of some of these poems.

ABOUT THE AUTHOR

Tim Bowling has published numerous poetry collections, including *Low Water Slack*; *Dying Scarlet* (winner of the Stephan G. Stephansson Award for Poetry); *Darkness and Silence* (winner of the Canadian Authors Association Award for Poetry); *The Witness Ghost* and *The Memory Orchard* (both nominated for the Governor General's Literary Award); and his *Selected Poems* (winner of the Robert Kroetsch City of Edmonton Book Prize). Bowling's work in poetry and prose has been honoured with two Canadian Authors Association Awards; two Writers Trust of Canada nominations; a Guggenheim Fellowship; five Alberta Book Awards; the Acorn-Plantos People's Poetry Award; and a Roderick Haig Brown Award nomination. Bowling served as the 2015 Canadian judge for the Griffin International Poetry Prize.

PHOTO CREDIT: JACQUELINE BAKER